Beyond the
A Guide to Runic Divination

by Paul Sykes

www.capallbann.co.uk

Beyond the Yew Dale

©Copyright THE LITTLE BLACK DOG 2004

ISBN 186163 183 9
First published as a limited edition, June 1993
Reprinted and revised, November 1994
Reprinted and revised, December 1998
This edition published 2004

ALL RIGHTS RESERVED

No part of this publication may be reproduced, stored in a retrieval system or transmitted in any form or by any means, electronic, mechanical, photocopying, scanning, recording or otherwise without the prior written permission of the author and the publisher.

Cover design by Paul Mason
Cover and internal illustrations by Matthew Powell

Published by:

Capall Bann Publishing
Auton Farm
Milverton
Somerset
TA4 1NE

Contents

Introduction	1
1 Runic Soul	7
2 Norse Mythology	13
3 Rune Meanings	23
Summary	75
Spreads and Casts	77
Runecasts	79
Rune Spreads	85
Advanced Divination	91
Glossary	97
Bibliography	101
Appendix 1	102
Appendix 2	103
Appendix 3 Pronunciation Guide	104

Introduction

With the ever-growing awareness of our Northern heritage the runes are becoming a popular form of divination., that is entwined with the concept of 'wyrd'. An undefinable but ever present force that affects all our actions and thoughts. Thereby using the runes as a form of divination they can be used to our benefit as once our ancestors did.

Its origins however are buried in the mists of time, when man was still colonising the newly formed forests and swamps left by the retreating Ice sheets throughout much of Northern Europe. Towards the equator however in Egypt and what is now modern Ethiopia, vast areas were periodically inundated by vast floods, creating a time of trade and war. Migrations were rife and caused many exchanges of ideas, language and technology, until the beginning of the Sumerian and Egyptian civilisations brought about some stability.

The theories presented so far do not explain how a language that takes many hundreds of years to mature appeared at the same time, or possibly earlier than the languages like Etruscan and Latin, and yet was supposed to have originated from them. Inscriptions that have been found in the Scandinavian area that are dated to before 50BCE suggesting that the culture and language had already been established for at least several hundred years before this date. The origins of the runic futhark therefore need to be looked for elsewhere and with different concepts in mind, we find that a number of proto scripts have helped to resolve some of the mystery.

Sinai	English	Sabean	Sinai	English	Sabean
𓁹	ʼ	𐩠	ע	ṣ	𐩮
𐡁	b	𐩨	8	q	𐩤
⌐	g	𐩴	ᑫ	r	𐩧
𐤃	d	𐩵	ω	š	𐩦
𐤄	h	𐩢	†	t	𐩩
𐤅	w	𐩥		s	𐩯
=	z	𐩸		ḥ	𐩡
𐤇	ḥ	𐩣		ś	𐩽
𐤈	ṭ	𐩷		f	𐩰
ω	k	𐩫		ḍ	𐩳
ℓ	l	𐩡		ġ	𐩶
∼	m	𐩣		ṭ	𐩷
𐤍	n	𐩬		ḏ	𐩹
⊙	ʿ	○		ṯ	𐩻
⌒	p	𐩲		ẓ	𐩼

Fig. 1a

The hallstringar script originates from Northern Europe in the Bronze age, and is often quoted as the forerunner of the Elder Futhark. This is a strong possibility but it has only symbols that relate to the Aesir, the Sky Gods. To find the fertility symbols that are prevalent in runic we must look to the south where during the Bronze Age, North Africa was a very fertile land, especially around the Nile Delta. A land peopled by Gods, pyramids and the Sphinx, and to the southeast near the source of the Nile a country known as Axum, now modern day Ethiopia.

Here we find more monuments and inscriptions at least 1000 yrs BCE, where the language is Sabean, and its similarity to the fertility symbols in the Elder Futhark is uncanny. There is also proof through the sagas that a race of gods known as the Vanir warred with the Aesir but eventually traded and settled down to peace in a land to the west. This is most likely Russia and Finland were the final pieces of Runic would have been gathered, probably by one of the wandering nomadic tribes that were the indigenous population of that area. Their knowledge mostly forgotten from when their ancestors lived so far to the south in Axum. The mythology however survived but was altered into poetic forms, e.g. The story of a flood caused by the killing of the Giant Ymir by Odhinn and his brothers, harking back to their memories of the great glacial melts that would of caused extensive flooding around the Nile Delta.

The Hallstringar and Sabean scripts play a prominent role in forming the Elder Futhark as is illustrated, but it is the race memories that have given us the rich tapestry mythological ideas and tales from this era.

The Elder Futhark is the oldest of the three main runic scripts, the other two variants are the Younger Futhark and the Anglo Saxon Futhark. All of which take the first six letters as the name for the language.

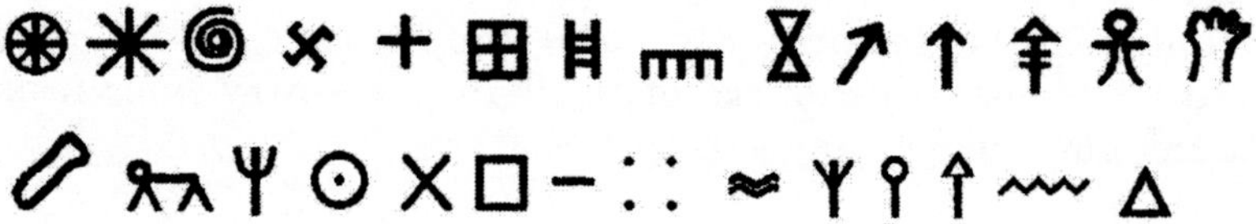

⊕ ✳ ◎ ✗ + ⊞ Ħ ▥ ⌛ ↗ ↑ ⚷ 𝌂 ⼻
⫽ ⚹ Ψ ⊙ ✕ ☐ - ∷ ≈ Ψ ⚲ ⇧ ∿ △

Fig. 1b

ᚠᚢᚦᚨᚱᚲᚷᚹᚺᚾᛁᛃᛇᛈᛉᛊᛏᛒᛖᛗᛚᛜᛟᛞ
f u th a r k g w h n i y ei p z s t b e m l ng o d

Fig. 1c

F: ᚠ, U: ᚢ, Th: ᚦ, A: ᚨ, R: ᚱ, K: ᚲ

Runic is a versatile language that gives a name to each rune and is divided into sets of eight, known as aetts each of which has practical and magical significance. These are known as Freya's eight, Hagalls eight and Tyr's eight respectively in the Elder Futhark. The Younger Futhark did not have the same divisions as it was purely used as a language. The Anglo Saxon Futhark was divided up into a number of divisions as well as having a name assigned to each rune, it unfortunately has a lot of differences that would require to much space to go into within this publication. It is for this reason that I have stayed with the Elder Futhark as system of divination, but it can be applied to the other Futharks with a little forethought.

1
Runic Soul

Before looking at the Mythology surrounding these people we must look at their souls. Thereby creating a new type of reading based on these ideas and the inherent numerology that is based on the runic system (the relevant spread is given at the end of the chapter on rune spreads and casts). To understand their state of mind the following scenario was written using the historical facts at hand and a little imagination.

A cold vicious wind swept across the bleak moorland, only broken in it's course by a small mound of earth giving scant shelter to a small group of frightened villagers. The shaman raised his hands once more to utter the words of power, and carefully traced the final rune symbols, sealing the tomb for all time. The villagers feeling safe now, shuffled back to their huts and warm fires. Following a different trail the shaman trudged through the gorse, wearily towards the next village.

The above scene embodies some aspects of the more formal duties of a Vitki however the death rites although important, often took second place to the rites of a seer.

The runes were used constantly throughout the Viking age and well beyond and nearly everyone knew something of them and as a consequence they were used as a language, for divination, warding against detrimental forces, death rites, merchants tokens etc.

It was often left to travelling shamans male or female to foretell the future, and to skalds to sing and write down the sagas. On an everyday level, runes were carved into memorial stones e.g. a stone was raised to the death of a man who had set out to join Cnut's armies in England, but never made it past Jutland, the extract of which follows

Djarf and Urokja and Vigi and Jogeir and Geirhjalm, all brothers, had this stone raised in memory of Svein, their brother. He died in Jutland, but was to have gone to England. May God and God's mother aid his spirit and soul better than his own acts did.

There are many such stones raised to commemorate those who died in battle, building a bridge, even to a faithful wife. These monuments are to be found all over Sweden, Norway and Denmark, and represent a valuable source of runic information. In addition to these rune stones it was common practice to carve a rune or runes onto weapons, jewellery, boxes and the gateposts of houses. Some had magical significance others plain ornamentation or even just a makers mark. Often poles of insult were erected against an enemy and were known as 'nidhing poles'.

In general the runes were very versatile and as a living language they did not escape change, so that by the year 800CE the Elder Futhark evolved to become the Younger Futhark consisting of 16 runes. The mainstay of the language was however not in the runes but in the oral tradition of the Norse peoples, so that the longer texts were not written down until the language started to use Latin script instead of Runes, relegating them to become a dying language after about 1200CE and used only for trading counters and magical purposes thereafter.

The Norse peoples had strong religious convictions that the runes were a major part of, as well as beliefs that relate to how they viewed magic, death and the soul. Working inwards from our outermost level the first term we come across is the Lich. This is the physical body and is the outward manifestation of all the other aspects combined, and relates to the exterior nature of the person under normal conditions. The Hamr is the emotional or Astral body and acts as a vessel for the life-force/soul and was capable of leaving the physical body during dreaming. The Minni and Hugr are our memory and thoughts respectively and with the Hamingja which is our personal power source and were the life-force originates from, they form aspects of the Astral body. The diagram on the next page is an illustration of these thoughts.

The fetch or fylga is a reflection of our Anima or Animus, and can often appear as a female or animal shape, representing the collective hamingja of our ancestors. It is accessed through our Minni and is futher expanded in a psychological reading, details of which are given in a later chapter.

Divination can be thought of as a way to look into our fate, at the present or into the future. Fate can however in the Norse world be defined in two distinct ways.

Orlog is the impersonal wyrd of mankind and is very nearly impossible to avoid. On the personal level each of us has what is called a web of wyrd and is alterable or worked around with an effort of willpower.

The term wyrd was thought of as an event from the past, affecting the present and laying shadows into the future. Each layer becomes finer as it goes towards our future and is more capable of change. The idea of which is embodied in the runes Perthro, Hagalaz, Nauthiz and Isa and is futher enhanced by their connections with the three Norns.

Thus giving us the three layers of wyrd that is represented by the three Norns.

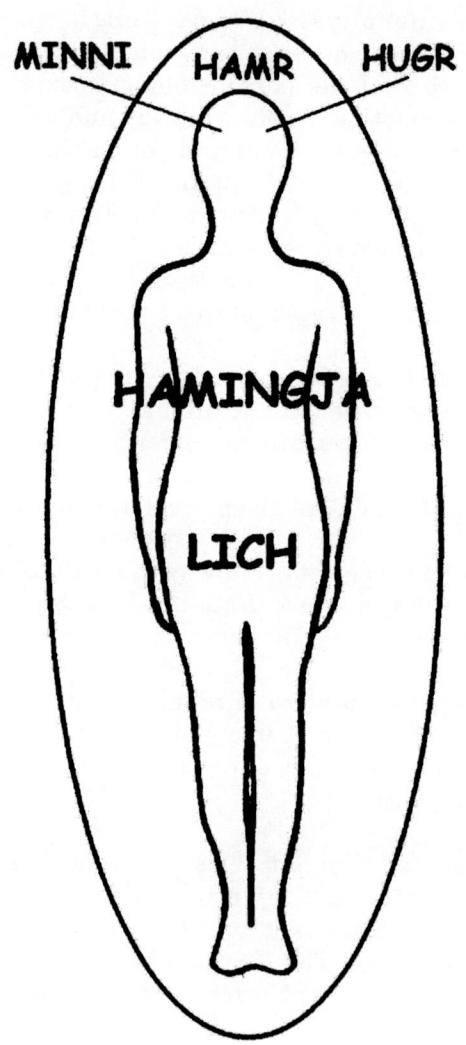

Fig. 2

Urd - That which was
Verdhandi - That which is now
Skuld - That which is to become

So that by following these principles we come to understand the web of wyrd, and can breathe life into our readings. The fabric that is woven by ourselves can then be looked upon as a story of our life.

2
Norse Mythology

Creation Myth

To know the Gods of Norse Mythology we must look to their origins, when only two states of matter existed. Muspellheimr, the realm of all consuming fire and Nifleheimr, the realm of stillness and ice. Ginnungap the great void seperated these two realms, but not completely as an interchange of opposing energy occurred, creating the first river composed of milky ice.

The river wore away steadily at the great blocks of ice on Nifleheimr's rim, revealing the cow Audmula. Licking the salty blocks of ice for nourishment she uncovered a massive ice giant, Ymir who in turn fed upon her milk.

From the giants sweat the first gods were formed, who were known as Odhinn, Vili and Ve. Their outrage of the evil Ymir eventually led to his death. So that his flesh was shaped into the Earth, his blood the salt seas, his bones the fells, his hair the forests, then raising Ymir's skull aloft they created the sky and from his brains the clouds. Odhinn set four dwarves to hold the skull and they were named Nordri, Austri, Sudri and Vestri.

Later the first man and woman were made from an ash and an elm, and were so named Aska and Embla. From Muspelheimr Odhinn caught two sparks, casting them aloft to form the sun and moon. Sol and Mani controlled them and likewise these two Gods were chased by two wolves until the end of time. From this time onwards, other events and wars dictated the creation of the other realms.

Aesir and Vanir

The Aesir or warrior/sky gods settled in Asgardhr, the highest realm. Odhinn and his wife Frigga together with his companions Thorr the thunderer and Tyr watched and guided the young Earth. Other gods settled here also, but Heimdallr and Baldur were not as well known, unlike Loki who is well chronicled as the adversary. They were joined later after a costly war with the Vanir, by Freyr and Freya, brother and sister who were fertility gods, but are counted amongst the warriors also.

Odhinn

Odhinn was known as the Allfather of the gods in Asgardhr, and although not worshipped as widely as Thorr, he was feared by the Norse for his fickleness over life and death. He often travelled the Nine worlds taking many different names and guises. The many aspects of his personality earned him the reputation of deviousness and as a mischief maker, often his behaviour echoing that of Loki.

During the ordeal of hanging from the world tree for nine days and nights, wounded by his own spear, he gained the wisdom of the runes. The sacrifice was then completed by giving an eye to the Etin Mimir, who after his subsequent death guarded the well of inspiration in the realm of Jotunheimr. From Frigga his wife he acquired the knowledge of Seidhr-magic.

He is often to be seen as a tall man with a grey beard, and a broad rimmed hat pulled over his missing eye, and travels the worlds on Sleipnir. Also to be found by his side are two ravens, Huginn and Muninn, his eyes to the other worlds. He is also frequently seen with two wolves, his Guardians.

Frigga

An important goddess in the heirachy, and Odhinn's wife, she sat counsel with him and was well versed in seidh and rune lore. Only Odhinn would she tell if her counsel was asked for, in this she was quite adamant. She also had a number of hand maidens who helped her to complete her many tasks in her role as the Goddess of marriage. Each handmaiden could also, like Odhinn be seen as aspects of the same Goddess. For as the mistress of magic she was known by the name Saga.

Yngvi Freyr

The brother of Freya, he is a god of fertility and war, and is associated with the rune Ingwaz. Together Freyr and Freya rule Ljossalfheimr and are of the Vanir. Freyr was often pulled in a cart as an effigy in spring around the land to secure a good harvest, often accompanied by a chosen female. Freyr also has a cart which is drawn by two boars.

Freya

The goddess of love and fertility, and sister to Yngvi Freyr. Freya is Odhinn's magical consort and as such has the right to claim half the slain that come to Valhalla. She is known by many names in a similar way to Odhinn. Popular names for Freya were Gullveig, Heidh the Witch, Heithrun, Syr, Vanadis etc. Freya took many lovers and was even reputed to have slept with her own brother Freyr. Her abode is the hall Folkvengr and has a chariot drawn by two large cats.

Tyr

Known as the god of war and justice, his name was used in battle to bring victory, and the rune Tiwaz was inscribed onto sword hilts as a potent symbol of victory.

His love and sense of justice did not however fare him well when the wolf Fenris became unmanageable and the gods decided to bind him. For it was only by using the magical cord Gleipnir that this task could be accomplished. The wolf however required an act of trust on behalf of the gods as he was unsure that he could break free from this third binding. Thus Tyr offered his right hand which the wolf took on finding that he could not break free from this strange cord.

Tyr was an earlier sky god who was superseded by Odhinn, and can be found clothed in red and carrying a sword as a symbol of Justice.

Thorr

Thorr was a popular god amongst the common people as his simple life and ways, mirrored there own. His popularity extended to Asgardhr as his success against the continual threat of the giants earned him much respect. He matched most of the giants in size and strength and with the help of his magical hammer Mjollinir he was unbeatable. The noise of his encounters with the giants and the sparks caused by his hammer, associated him with thunder and lightning and he came to be known as the Thunderer.

Physically he was tall and well muscled with a long red beard. He journeyed in a chariot drawn by two goats, Tanngnjost (tooth-gnasher) and Tanngrisnir (tooth-gritter).

Baldur

A typical Sun God whose main claim to fame was his invulnerability, which came about when a dream foretelling of Baldur's death was not accepted by Frigga. She made everything forswear not to harm Baldur, but did not think to ask the lowly mistletoe. This became Baldur's undoing, when Loki fashioned an arrow from the mistletoe, thus killing the mighty Baldur. Seen dressed in white and as bright as the sun.

Heimdallr

The origins of Heimdallr are very obscure, as the rune poem (*Heimdaligaldr*) was mainly lost and only fragments of it exist. He was thought to be one of the Aesir but shares the Vanic wisdom of foresight.

He is able to hear to hear all that happens within the nine realms, and is the guardian of the Rainbow bridge bifröst. At Ragnarok he will signal the final battle by blowing the horn Gjallarhorn. Being the highest and brightest of the gods he is cloaked in white.

Loki

A mischievous trickster god who was rarely helpful and sometimes pure evil. Loki represents uncontrolled fire the anathema of Heimdallr. The exploits of Loki were famous throughout the nine worlds and were sometimes helpful in the end to the other gods. One such episode during the building of the wall around Asgard, Loki shapeshifted to a Mare and gave birth to Sleipnir. Later exploits caused untold trouble especially a mating to the Giantess Angrboda from which Jormungand the world serpent, Fenris the wolf and Hel the ruler of the dead were born.

His list of crimes became so great that he was captured and bound to a rock with venom dripping onto his face from a snake above him, and there he would stay until Ragnarok.

Mimir

Known to have originated from a race of Etin's. They were of a wise disposition but similar in form to the Giants.

During the war between the Aesir and Vanir he was given to the Vanir as a hostage and killed. Odhinn kept Mimir's head which became associated with the well situated in Jotunheimr and was afterwards known as Mimir's well. It is the well of creative inspiration.

Three Norns

The three Norns are known as goddesses of fate. They weave the web of wyrd that controls the life of men, Urd representing the past, Verdhandi the present and Skuld the future.

The past has gone
The present is now
The future is our wyrd

The Norns are to be found at the three aspects of the well, were the roots of Yggdrasil take nourishment. They are to be found in Nifleheimr, under Asgardhr and in Jotunheimr. Of which this seems to be the most important and is known as the well of Mimir, or the well of inspiration.

The Nine Worlds

The Norse believed that their world Midgardhr was one of Nine such worlds. Starting with Asgardhr the highest world, Midgardhr in the centre and hel in the lowest reaches. Immediately above Midgardhr is Ljossalfheimr and surrounding it are the elemental worlds Nifleheimr, Muspelheimr, Jotunheimr, and Vanaheimr, with Svatalfheimr just below.

ASGARDHR	realm of the gods - Valhalla
LJOSSALFHEIMR	world of light - light elf world
MIDGARDHR	middle earth - material plane
SVARTALFHEIMR	realm of darkness - dark elf world
NIFLEHEIMR	realm of ice - north
MUSPELHEIMR	realm of fire - south
VANAHEIMR	realm of water - Vanir world, west
JOTUNHEIMR	realm of chaos - world of giants,
HEL	realm of stillness - death

Rainbow Bridge
This is the bridge that crosses between Midgardhr and Asgardhr. It is composed of three elements, Fire(red), Air(blue), and Water(green). The bridge is guarded by the god Heimdallr.

World Tree
Within Norse mythology a great tree passes through all nine realms, and is known as the World Tree. It is referred to as an Ash tree as well as an evergreen and is therefore likely to encompass many different trees.

It is said that the Dragon Nidhogg gnaws the root in Nifleheimr, deer and goats feed on the branches and the squirrel Ratatosk runs up and down the trunk passing messages between Nidhogg and an Eagle that lives in the highest branches.

3
Rune Meanings

The runes are at times elusive in their understanding. This is overcome by going back to the meaning given in the rune name and working from it, to build a conceptual idea based on the mythology surrounding the runes.

Wounded I hung on a wind-swept gallows
For nine long nights,
Pierced by a spear, Pledged to Odhinn
Offered, myself to myself;
The wisest know not from whence spring
The roots of that ancient rood.

They gave me no bread, They gave me no mead;
I looked down; with a loud cry
I took up runes; from that tree I fell.

Nine lays of power I learned from the famous
Bolthor, Bestla's father;
He poured me a draught of precious mead,
Mixed with magic Ohdrerir.

Learned I grew then, lore-wise,
Waxed and throve well:
Word from word gave words to me,
Deed from deed gave deeds to me.

Better not to ask than to overpledge
As a gift that demands a gift,
Better not to send than to slay to many.

To learn to sing them, Loddfafnir,
Will take you a long time,
Though helpful they are if you understand them,
Useful if you use them,
Needful if you need them.

Havámal (Words of the high One)

This then is the essentials of runecraft, it holds many secrets, not all are apparent, allowing the rune interpretations in the following section to take the above passage from the *Poetic Edda* into account as well as the previous chapter on mythology. There are also a number of subdivisions where the runes can be split into groups of three. They are known respectively as Freya's aett, Hagall's aett and Tyr's aett.

Freya's aett represents runes that describe the formation of the nine worlds and the preconcious ideas that underly the other runic layers to come. It starts with the rune Fehu that is the fire of Muspelheimr, followed by the rune Uruz, that represents the cow Audhmula, as she formed from the ice of Nifleheimr as it slowly melted. This reasoning can be futher applied to other runes and the creation myth.

Hagall's aett is not the name of a god or goddess but a force of nature i.e. hailstones, but is also the rune of the past. Again this layer follows the creation myth with the runes Isa and Sowilo representing the ice of Nifleheimr and the fertilising and warming energy of the sun.

The last aett is Tyr's which is only right as he appears to of been one of the original gods and is well known for his sacrifice, thus showing a higher more spiritual nature of man. Thus this final layer shows the vitues that man should endeavor to reach, ending with the rune Dagaz, the dawn, as the cycle completes itself and begins anew.

Fehu
Meaning: Cattle
Colour: Orange

As Fehu is the first rune of the Elder Futhark, and the creation myth is correspondingly the birth of Norse mythology, it is appropriate to refer to it in context of this rune.

Audmula a great cow was the first living being that came from the rime ice of Nifleheimr. This is important as the root meaning of Fehu is cattle, and in relation to the Nomadic tribes of the time it represented a form of mobile wealth i.e. a bartering system. This was later replaced by gold as feudal system began to take shape.

As Fehu is the first rune, Dagaz or daylight is the last, and as such brings its light to bear on the gold, allowing tongues of flame to flicker within it, reminding us of its primeval origins. Thus Fehu is the uncontrolled fire that is our very being. This is again echoed in the saga of the sea god Aegir, whose great undersea halls were lit by gold from shipwrecks, and was known as Aegirs fire,

Following the interconnections between the runes and Norse mythology a circle of runic knowledge and inheritance is formed, which within Fehu is represented by a union of opposites leading to fulfilment within oneself.

Notes: Wealth, especially mobile wealth i.e. a horse or a cart, Primeval fire, A union of opposites, Fulfilment.

Uruz
Meaning: Wild Auroch
Colour: Green

ᚢ

The primeval nature of Uruz is exemplified by the Wild Auroch, a species of Wild Bison. The strength and vitality of these creatures led to a great challenge for the hunter, especially the first time, when it was often used as a form of initiation to classify him as a man amongst his tribe. When used in divination it can often represent a challenge that can only be overcome through a strength of purpose. In a similar way to the strength card in the Tarot.

In matters of health, Uruz will indicate good health when associated with other positive runes such as Sowilo. Or a need to take care when the runes Hagalaz or Isa are present.

On a basic level the rune shape symbolises the horns of the Auroch or a later interpratation, a horseshoe. It is with the latter in mind, that the luck brought by a horseshoe can be positive or negative and is often enhanced depending on our mood. It is therefore of importance to keep a positive frame of mind at all times lest we indulge.

Notes: Primeval nature, Strength and vitality, Strength of purpose, Good health or a need to be careful, Initiation, luck can be positive or negative.

Thurisaz
Meaning: Giant,Thorn
Colour: Red

Like most of the runes this one contains the root word that allows its meaning to be interpreted quite easily, and its connection with fire and ice is also apparent. For the purposes of divination we can start with the word Thurse which in English means Giant.

Thorr is the giant referred to here as he was in stature and birth much akin to the giants he defended Asgardhr against. His destructive nature and fiery battles leads us to the way in which all actions using Thurisaz should be viewed. This led him to being popular amongst the common people, and to be a god to be relied upon in times of need.

The powerful nature of Thurisaz can be tempered physically by an internal understanding of the rune shape. Where the runes Kenaz and Isa or fire and ice respectively can lead to very personal spiritual changes.

Within the Anglo Saxon rune script this rune was known as Thorn which is from the hawthorn bush, and was used to prick the senses into awakening.

Thorr was married to the corn goddess Sif and his hammer Mjollnir is symbolised by the rune. Again this leads us back to the rune Kenaz. So that Thorr was more than just a warrior god with the people, it was his efforts on their behalf that brought fertility. And when found with other runes such as Jera or Berkano it is assured.

Notes: Destruction, Rapid changes, Awakening of the self, Fertility in all forms but especially physical.

Ansuz
Meaning: God, Odinn
Colour: Deep Blue

ᚨ

When we associate the root word of Ansuz with that of our higher self, known as the Holy Guardian Angel in Quabalistic work, we find it as a Godform, specifically that of Odhinn. It is the communication from this that can take many forms, inwardly it is known as Ohdrehir, or poetic inspiration, outwardly a letter, telephone call or as simple as talking to some one.

Ohdrerir brings our intuition to the surface creating original thought. It can take a number of forms that depends on the surrounding runes i.e. Kenaz for creativity or Mannaz for social gatherings.

In the myths, Odhinn was Lord of the Wild Hunt, which occurred around midnight to the early hours before dawn. Most especially around the winter solstice, where night is longer than day. Thus within divination Ansuz can be related to around midnight or the winter solstice.

Notes: Communication with the higher self, Ohdrerir, Original thought, Physical communication by letter etc, Time of midnight or winter solstice.

Raidho
Meaning: Cart, Sunwheel
Colour: Yellow/Red

A cart was a common mode of transport when any distance was involved or a load to be moved. It could be pulled by horses but more often as not by oxen. Being a planned journey, difficulties were to be expected, often leading to a broadening of ones experience.

In the mythology of the Norse the sun was taken across the sky in a chariot guided by Sol. Thus being known as the sunwheel. Raidho was therefore related to relative time according to the position of the sun during the day, and at the winter solstice were Raidho is a counterpart to Ansuz.

When Raidho is taken in association with Ehwaz the horse it signifies the final planned journey. The timing of this will be related to the surrounding runes. In essence any journey may make us consider our mortality and how we should move forward to meet it with no regrets, after all it was planned.

Notes: Planned journey, Relative time in accordance with the sun, Winter solstice, Final journey.

Kenaz
Meaning: Torch
Colour: Bright Red

A controlled fire such as a torch or campfire is at the root of what Kenaz is about. It describes mans first steps towards civilisation or conversely, away from nature. It has enhanced our material life but out of control it can destroy precious resources.

Under control Kenaz will burn away the dross within our life, or in poor health it will clear away negativity that led to it.

In respect of Kenaz as a torch, its light will attract insects i.e. moths, and used with our inner fire this leads to a symbolic if not a physical attraction to the opposite sex. This expression could then lead to procreativity which is at the centre of Kenaz's divinatory meaning.

On a more earthly level the controlled fire leads to creativity when employed by a smith. This relates to its use by the dark elves in the realm of Svartalfheimr.

The campfire is only lit when darkness approaches and in the summer this can be as late as ten o clock, as such this is worth considering when trying to relate the when of an event.

Notes: Controlled fire leading to constructive or destructive events, Burning away the dross or need to do so, Sexual attraction, Procreativity, Time of campfire as night approaches.

Gyfu
Meaning: Gift, Sacrifices
Colour: Brown/Green

With Gyfu the importance of giving, or the receiving of a gift should not be taken lightly. May it be from the Gods, a friend, a partner etc, and is given in complete trust, so that no reward should be expected. The sacrifice could be as simple as a vow.

By receiving a gift their can be no obligation felt to return such as this would be a breach of trust. Only if you truly want to can the rightness be brought into being.

In the creation myth there is reference to the first human beings, Aska and Embla who through Odhinn and his brothers Vili and Ve were given life. The union of the Ash and Elm as signified by the shape of Gyfu became a form of sacrifice to Odhinn and Asgardhr. This is why it is used to represent a kiss on letters etc.

Relating these ideas Gyfu is a powerful marker in divination where relationships are concerned. The need for sacrifice will indicate how the relationship is, or how it will continue, or not depending on what is offered.

Notes: Gift, Sacrifice, Partnerships, The need to sacrifice to preserve.

Wunjo
Meaning: Joy, Harmony
Colour: Gold

ᚹ

Harmony comes from a joy within and is a profoundness found in Wunjo. It is from the joy of bringing the inner and outer selves together that harmony is created. Within any cast Wunjo is always viewed as positive as it represents the querents True Will.

Depending on the surrounding runes his or her ability to act in accordance with it, will be determined. In essence Wunjo represents a wish that you would like to manifest on the material level.

In Tacitus's *Germania* their is a reference to Glory sticks, pieces of Hazel wood with runic symbols etched into their surfaces and used for divination. This I feel refers to the glory that one would feel by knowing oneself, divination being one method by which this could occur.

Wunjo is a fire rune in so much as it is the feminine light of sol that illuminates the moon and ourselves. Connecting the female and male leading to a partnership that is physical and spiritual. This is completed in the Mannaz rune.

The cycle of the Sun and Moon can be seen at sunset, so that Wunjo can be associated with sunset when using it in a cast.

Notes: Harmony from within, Joy of self, True will, Union by connection of male and female, Partnership on equal terms. Sunset.

Hagalaz
Meaning: Hailstones
Colour: Grey

ᚺ

A combination of the disruptive force that is caused by a shower of hailstones, and the beauty of the ice crystals that are hailstones, typifies the complex nature of Hagalaz when used for divination. Representing as it does a naturally disruptive external force that becomes life-giving as its subsequent melting occurs, and thus completing the cycle of nature.

The *Poetic Edda* describes a realm known as netherhel or the realm of the dead, which the rune Hagalaz describes, especially in connection with the goddess Hel whose upper body is that of a beautiful woman and her lower half a rotting corpse. It is the wisdom of the past, that used properly can be beneficial over the long term. Though at the moment it is unavoidable and disruptive. These events could only have been avoided if action had been taken at an earlier date. Also mentioned in the eddas are the Norns and the well of Hverglmir in Netherhel, and therefore associates Hagalaz with past events as the rune Eihwaz can be.

The importance of this rune cannot be overstated and a deeper understanding of it will allow many levels of wyrd to be explored

Notes: Rapid disruption, cleansing, wisdom from the past. Personal change due to impersonal circumstances. Connections to the past when wyrd is involved.

Nauthiz
Meaning: Need, Necessity
Colour: Red

A change of circumstances in our lives will often cause constraints and limitations. This could be through the impersonal events caused by Hagalaz or on a personal level by Thurisaz, creating the needfire within us that will shape our futures, by burning away the shackles and revealing our true path.

This occurs periodically to avoid a condition of stasis that would create a spiritual or mental death, and allows us to touch our true will, and how to achieve it.

The knowledge gained in completion of this task lets us move past the present and to look to the future. It is a form of wisdom that is found at the well of Mimir in the realm of Jotunheimer, and were the Norn Skuld, weaver of the future dwells.

The essential nature of Nauthiz is therefore to form a needfire/necessity within us to overcome obstacles to give a glimpse of the future and the path we try stay on.

Notes: Needfire, necessity, delays and constraints leading to future freedom, and strength of mind.

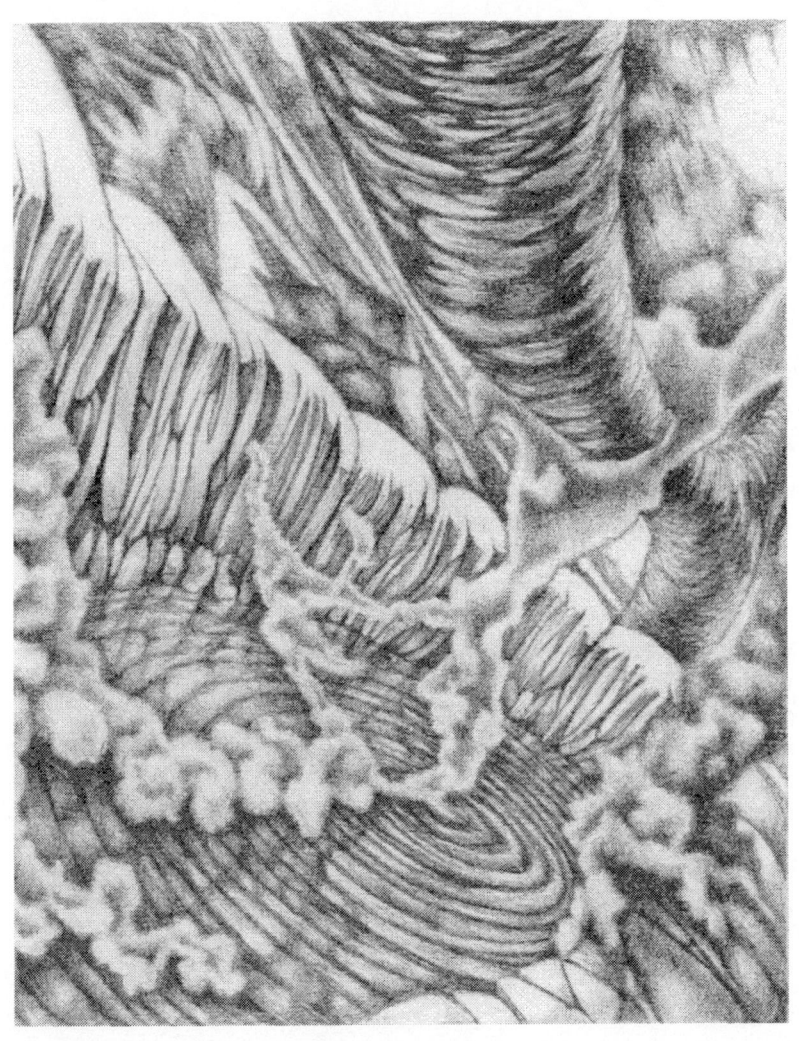

Isa
Meaning: Ice
Colour: White

The primeval nature of Isa comes from the realm of Nifleheimr, a world composed entirely if ice, It is the basis from which all the other realms were created when it interacted with sparks from Muspelheimr. Its edges began to melt forming great rivers of milk and blocks of ice, one of which formed into a great cow Audmula, and from another the ice giant Ymir.

The stasis represented by the ice is the form used by the Norn Verdhandi who works to create the present, making it solid. This can only be transformed by the application of fire, the creative spark. Thus from a union of Fire and Ice the present can be made to work for us, not against us.

Isa can be seen in a positive light when it acts to guide us to live each day to its fullest, from moment to moment and not to wander around seeing only clouds and impossible visions. Its very purity and coldness can be beautiful to some, but disruptive where relationships are concerned. Often indicating a cooling of the essential essence that is needed. On a personal level though it can purify and cleanse allowing positive energy to be accessed.

Notes: Stasis, delays, living in the present. Beauty, cooling of relationships, purifying of the self.

Jera
Meaning: Harvest, Year
Colour: Yellow

To understand Jera we must consider what it conveyed to the Norse people. To them the it was more than just describing the year, it was the most fruitful part of the Year, the time of Harvest, a gathering of crops before winter. The fulfilment of ones efforts over time. In human terms the birth of a child, but both requiring a period of fallow to recover. Thus the human cycle matched the yearly cycle of nature, and the gods became archetypes for the people, especially Thorr and his wife Sif. Between them they represented the fertility of the land and the harvest from it.

The harvest is the symbol of the land and the realm is known as Midgardhr, the central realm and Jera is the centre rune of the Futhark. Jera therefore leads to fulfilment but only after a long steady natural cycle. Thus in terms of human fertility it is significant mainly when other fertility runes are present such as Berkano, Kenaz or Ingwaz. Importantly though Jera does not allow events to be forced, that they must happen in their own time.

Notes: Year, harvest, fertility on all levels, fulfilment. Events occurring naturally not forced.

Eihwaz
Meaning: Yew Tree
Colour: Green/Red

ᛇ

The Yew tree is a symbol of life and death, an evergreen that has a lifespan of over 1000yrs and yet its leaves, berries and wood are deadly poisonous.

Traditionally the yew was a source of wood for the English Longbow, which was used to great advantage as an offensive form of protection (i.e. Agincourt).

During the summer months when the sap evaporates, the toxins can cause hallucinations, leading to an awakening of the mind, that is of a very spiritual and personal experience. Mythologically the yew tree is to be found in the same dale as the well of Urdhr, the Norn concerned with the past. This is futher enhanced when the runes Perthro and Hagalaz are present, possibly indicating death in extreme circumstances.

Eihwaz occurs most often though in reference to offensive protection, physically or spiritually or the need to take action to protect oneself.

Notes: Life and death, longevity, offensive protection. Spiritual awakening, past events.

Perthro

Meaning: Lot Box
Colour: Black

Perthro embodies the mystery of the futhark and what it means to us. It is described in some references as a lot box i.e. a way to cast the dice of fate. A term more commonly known in Norse society as wyrd or orlog (see chapter one).

When it is used in conjunction with Isa, Nauthiz or Hagalaz it lets us determine the past or future occurrence of an event that is in our personal wyrd. One that could be difficult to avoid without foreknowledge, or an explanation of past events, to allow a greater insight.

On a more feminine level Perthro's shape gives us a key to its mysteries, where the water of life is found and the timelines are focused to form a new life. The birth of which is indicated by the rune Berkano.

Within a spread the appearance of either rune will suggest that there are hidden mysteries or secrets yet to be found. Their timing being dictated by the surrounding runes, such as Isa or Nauthiz.

Notes: Mysteries of the Futhark, fate or wyrd. Feminine secrets and hidden knowledge.

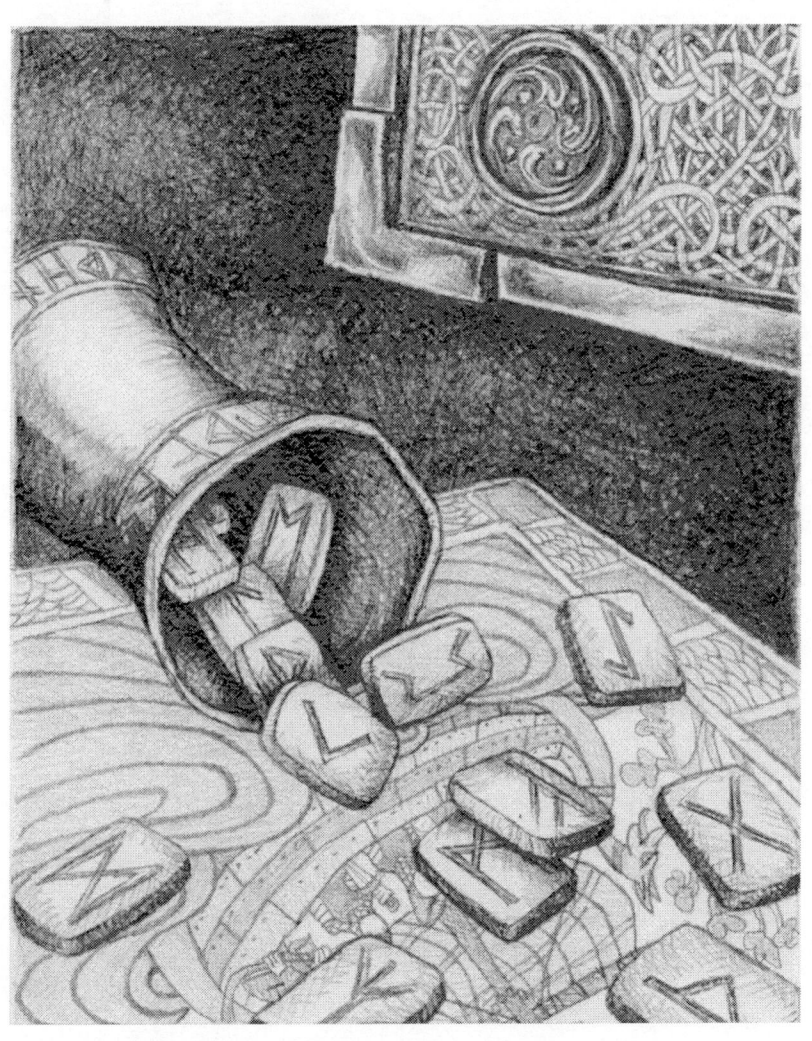

Elhaz
Meaning: Elk
Colour: Light Blue

Great herds of Elk once roamed the vast expanses, much like the Reindeer today. They had few predators who were able to harm them as a herd, but singly they were vulnerable.

The arms of Elhaz are the branches and the roots of the world tree that connects the higher and lower realms to Midgardhr. Like all trees it will sheild and protect those who need it and obscure our view just as easily.

In both cases Elhaz can lend its protection or stifle growth by obscuring the truth. To see this wisdom we must climb the branches of Yggdrasil to reach the higher realms, or cross the Rainbow bridge. This is guarded by the god Heimdallr and thus Elhaz is associated spiritual awakening and an understanding of the greater whole.

Notes: Defensive protection, obscuring the truth. Spiritual awakening and seeing the whole.

Sowilo
Meaning: Sun
Colour: Gold

The natural force of the sun when associated with a feminine influence has a nurturing and protective effect. This is unlike the transformative energy in the rune Dagaz.

Sowilo gives physical and spiritual growth leading to success, so often found in Goddess worship. Whereas its opposite and destructive effect is found only when the sun takes on a male form. Usually found in eastern civilisations such as Egypt or India.

The rising and setting of the sun each day became as important as the moon as a marker of time, during the day and the seasons. Especially so at the summer solstice where the goddess Sol was venerated. All of which is useful when using Sowilo in a runecast to understand the when of an event.

Notes: Feminine nurturing influence, protective strength, success. Relative time during daylight hours and great importance at the summer solstice.

Tiwaz
Meaning: God Tyr
Colour: Red

The runename Tiwaz, as with other runes is derived from the name of the god that it symbolises. Tyr/Tiw was originally a sky god who when superseded by Odhinn he became a warrior god, thus falling with the other Aesir gods.

The notoriety of Tyr comes from placing his right hand into the jaws of the wolf Fenris as an act of trust, whilst the other gods bound Fenris with the magical cord Gleipnir as a game of strength. The wolf, unable to free himself took Tyr's hand, leaving the god worse for wear. The courage to be found within the rune Tiwaz comes from this incident and should be seen as such when this rune is found in an otherwise negative reading. It can also be seen as foolishness or deception if the aspect of the wolf is present. This is unusual as Tyr was a warrior with impeccable courage and his rune was often used on a warrior's blade to assure them of success in the coming battle.

As a counterpart to Tyr we find the next rune Berkano is related to the Earthmother, thus we find that the male and female principle can be present when either rune comes up in a reading.

Notes: Courage and fortitude, with a sense of Justice. Victory against struggles. The male principle. Occasionally foolishness or deception.

Berkano
Meaning: Birch Tree
Colour: Green

The Silver Birch is a tall fast-growing tree with a white fungus covering the red bark. Thus the rune Berkano like the Birch tree will hide it's true nature from casual observation.

The trunk of the Birch was used in times past as the maypole and the twigs were bound together to form a birch that was used in fertility rites, to help expel negative forces and to bring fertility and growth to young couples. With relation to the rune shape its resemblance to the swollen breasts and womb of a pregnant woman futher adds to its mystery as a symbol of the Earth mother.

Although Berkano is thought of as a feminine rune, the concept of birth can represent the birth of new ideas that were previously hidden from us, and is as important to a woman as to a man. This hidden nature can also represent secrecy or deceit under certain circumstances, i.e. if the rune Hagalaz was to turn up.

Notes: Hidden nature. Clearing away of unwanted forces, Fertility, Pregnancy, Birth. New beginnings or ideas. Deceit hidden by a gloss.

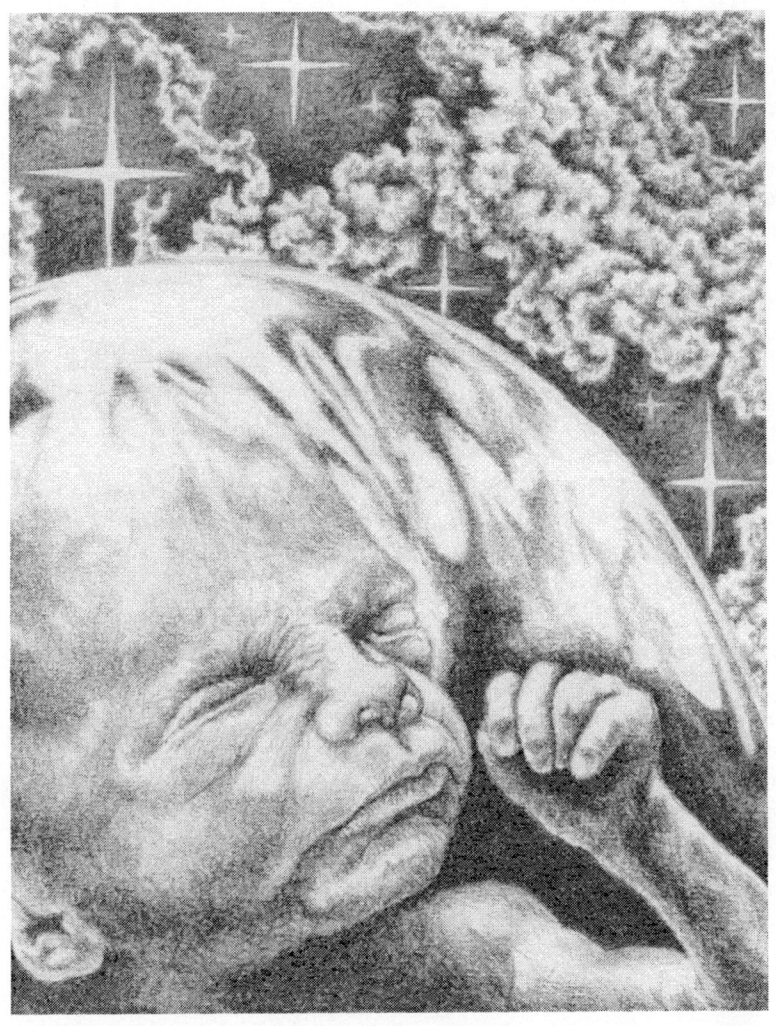

Ehwaz
Meaning: Horse
Colour: Green/Blue

M

In Northern Europe the horse was an important part of society, forming links between distant groups of people and its helpfulness in warfare. Thus creating a bond between man and his horse that over time gave the horse a mythical status. Such as Odhinn's steed Sleipnir whose ability to travel through different worlds was legendary.

The close association of horse and rider represents a duality that can be experienced on many levels of reality, and is often found in partnerships.

In some areas the horse played a direct part in divination as its moods and movements could be interpreted as omens for the future. Thus Ehwaz can allow knowledge that is normally un-available to be accessed.

With reference to the mythology, particularly the Poetic Edda and finds of horses in graves we know that the horse was thought to carry the dead to Valhalla. Therefore Ehwaz can with the relevant runes be considered as an indication of a death soon to occur.

Notes: Duality, Partnerships, Hidden knowledge in the form of omens, Last journey, Physical or Symbolic Travel.

Mannaz
Meaning: God Mannus, People
Colour: Silver

Mannaz represents an order or structure within society and how the individual relates to it. This social structuring is told of in a fragmentary poem about the God Heimdallr, who on his wanderings, fathers children from different levels of society, and thus determines their fates from then on.

Heimdallr is thought to be a younger form of the God Mannus, from whence the rune name Mannaz comes from. It is thought to help those who can be enlightened, to awake to their personal wyrd.

Mannaz is also related to Mani (possibly another form of the god Mannus) the moon god, which again relates to structure and rational thought. On a more personal level Mannaz is the deep harmony that is found when two people are together in a close relationship.

Such that Mannaz relates to your personal, or dual structure in a partnership or in relation to a society as a whole.

Notes: Social structure, inheritance, awakening of the self. Rationality of the moon. Harmony between individuals and groups.

Laguz
Meaning: Water
Colour: Light Blue

ᛚ

At this point in the futhark the outer meanings begin to mask the true concepts. As in the case of Laguz were the literal translation of water, that is feminine in nature, hides the masculine principle inherent in the rune shape. So that the emotions associated with the element of water is an outer principle combined with an inner masculine principle.

Thus a great range of emotions are found in a calm pool of tranquillity that is fed by a fast flowing river, whenever Laguz is in the runecast.

Laguz is also suggestive of the birthing waters, and could be indicative of an oncoming birth when the runes Jera and Berkano are present.

On a personal level, male or female, the cleansing effect of water can signal a clearing out of emotions, especially if fire runes proceed Laguz. It is generally a positive rune to have within a reading, unless badly aspected by runes such as Hagalaz.

Notes: Feminine/Masculine principle, with a range of emotions. To be one with the flow. Connections with birth. A personal or group cleansing effect.

Ingwaz
Meaning: God Freyr
Colour: Yellow/Green

In the rune Ingwaz we see the male principle deified in the form of the Vanir God of fertility, Yngvi Freyr. The rune is his seed, a gift, that is ready for transformation. Although its true meaning is to found in its shape, being representative of femininity and motherhood, and the doorway to conception and birth.

So finding Ingwaz with Berkano or Jera can indicate a physical birth yet to be conceived or to be born within the timespan of the reading.

The birth can be symbolic in the case of the male, but in either case it will often be a change for the better, after an appropriate transformation has occurred, allowing travel through the doorway to realms such as Vanaheimr or to other realms of physical reality.

Notes: Fertility, seed of transformation, femininity, pregnancy and birth. Transformative doorway leading to other realms of reality.

Othala
Meaning: Odal Land
Colour: Brown

The concept of Odal-land was derived the Teutonic tribes roaming as Nomads across much of Northern Europe, before settling as farmers. At which time the tribes concept of Ancestral Inheritance, in the form of children changed to become the area of land that a family or tribe could hold. Othala or Odal-land then became an enclosure to deter detrimental forces that could destroy the tribe.

The land was then passed on as inherited wealth when the children came of age, once more completing the cycle of genetic inheritance.

Othala is the result of the previous two runes Laguz and Ingwaz into the form of Ancestral Inheritance and should be interpreted with this in mind when it appears in a reading.

An enclosure can also act negatively by keeping in that which is struggling to free itself, or as someone who does not wish to see beyond his or her own boundary's.

Notes: Inherited wealth, within a tribal or family unit. Enclosure holding everything one owns. Blinkered mind.

Dagaz
Meaning: Day
Colour: Orange

The daylight that creates the dawn is the transformed energy of the sun. A female energy that has a restorative and fertilising effect upon the land, unlike the male solar divinity of eastern religions. That are often warlike and destructive.

With the heralding of the new dawn, their is victory over darkness, a rebirth. Often Dagaz represents a realisation that comes overnight, proceeded by a long period of gradual changes. It creates new patterns by growing and overcoming the old ones causing a correspondingly brighter future.

The circle of knowledge is now complete as Dagaz gives freely its transforming light to Fehu, causing the primeval fire to be kindled within it.

Dagaz is also associated with the triumph of summer over winter when new growth occurs, significantly when the day becomes longer after the winter solstice.

Notes: New dawn, causing transformation and growth creating patterns for a brighter future. Completion of a cycle.

Summary

In addition to the basic rune associations the rune order tells the story of creation e.g. Fehu is the creative fire of Muspelheimr, followed by the emergence of the cow Audmula from the ice, represented by the rune Uruz. The giant Ymir is given by Thurisaz, and is followed by Odhinn whose rune is Ansuz and his two brothers Vili and Ve. These associations continue throughout the entire futhark, thus enriching our knowledge of the futhark.

Other runes as mentioned have specific associations with ideas of wyrd, and represent the past ,present and future, as Hagalaz, Isa and Nauthiz respectively. They are bound together by the rune Perthro which embodies the idea of wyrd in its threefold aspect and can thus tell us much about a situation within a reading. It has on occasion been superseded by the blank rune, but this is unnecessary as it only complicates a system that works better without such an addition. Which historically never existed, except as an idea that embodied the whole Futhark.

I have therefore included a number of spreads and casts, some of which are original in concept to allow a greater choice for the purposes of divination. These are to be found in the next section as well as a section on advanced divination and Numerology.

Spreads and Casts

Divinatory Methods

This section on divination is about the practicalities of casting the runes and the spreads that can be used. With this in mind it is useful to refer to Tacitus a Roman historian who detailed a runecast that he witnessed in his journal *Germania*. It consisted of the caster laying out a white cloth, then quietly chanting to himself before dropping a number of glory sticks onto the cloth. He then picked three and gave his interpratation.

The glory sticks referred to were of hazel, but other woods especially fruit, such as apple have been mentioned in the Poetic Edda. The colour of cloth is probably optional also, though white seems to be a good neutral colour. Our other reference work must also be the *Poetic Edda*, especially the poem 'The words of the High One'.

The choice of material for the runes is a personal one, as references suggest that quite a variety of materials were used. Most often was wood, or fired clay and a colouring of blue or red for the runes. All aspects of the making were however done in a magical way using blood and breath to lend life to runes. As for carrying them a cloth or leather bag is preferable. It is not however essential to make either the bag or the runes oneself as this may be impracticable to do so, it is necessary though to add something of oneself to the magical tools one uses, such that some form of personal rite to cleanse and dedicate the runes to your purpose would be helpful.

On using them for divination it is wise to tell the gods what you are doing and to ask for their aid during the rite.

The following sections start with two original casts that are used for a futures reading and a general one respectively.

Runecasts

Futures Cast
The method for this cast is quite straight forward, as it involves holding all the rune staves in a cup or in the hand, phrasing the question and throwing the runes in a line in front of you. The cast can be used to determine a series of events fro 1 day to 1 year ahead, that the enquirer needs to know and could be of help to them. It is however not much use as a cast beyond a year as their is not enough detail provided.

Once the caster has cast the runes he will notice that some are laying face down, others are grouped together and are likely to be overlapping. The groups make up a series of events running from the present, (which are the runes closest to the caster i.e. the rune Isa in Fig 1), through Events 2-7 up to the rune Gyfu, Event 8,which is 1 year into the future.

If the first or last rune in the cast is face down, they are to be turned face up, as they determine the nature of the cast to be read and the beginning of the next cycle respectively. Any other runes however that are face down are not be read, but can influence any that they lay across, the rune that is partially covered is known as Murk (for more detail see *At the Well of Wyrd* by Edred Thorsson). The effect of this is to cause that rune to have a lessened or opposite effect and can influence the reading from that point onwards.

Reading
Although the rune Isa is shown face upwards in fig 1 it was face down in the original cast, the rune however is to be read as it indicates the starting point of this reading, thereby

FUTURES CAST

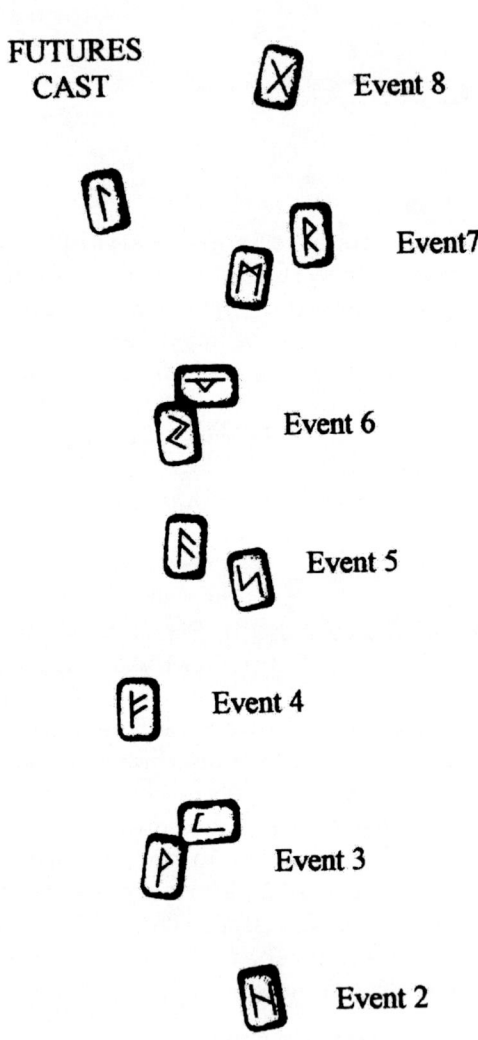

setting the tone of subsequent events. It represents a period of stasis at this point in his life and shows his inability to go forward.. This is then changed with the rune Hagalaz and shown as Event 2 in the cast. It causes a period of change lasting for about a month, which are outside of his control and are likely to be disruptive in nature. In event 3 we find that the rune Uruz is overlapping Wunjo, and reinforcing a feeling of despair combined with a lack of willpower. This however slowly changes until Event 4 is reached, where the rune Fehu describes the how his life becomes more fulfilling and leading to the runes Sowilo and Ansuz in Event 5.

The effect of which caused success combined with communication, leading to the next cycle of events with the runes Jera and Thurisaz in Event 6 These cause a new sequence of events leading to a meeting with people and travel, all of which creates a lot of emotions shown by the rune Laguz. This leads us to the last rune Gyfu in Event 8 which describes not so much an event but how he has learnt to cope with the years events, especially his emotional relationships.

This then is the basic concept of the cast, but as each one turns out radically different, intuition and experience will have to guide the reader when trying to interpret each new cast they do.

Nine Realms Cast

For this spread the runes are dropped to allow a cast similar to fig2b to form, and to be interpreted using the categories shown in fig2a. It follows that only the runes that have landed face up are to be read and in respect of the realm in which they have landed, a brief description of which follows.

Asgardhr Home of the gods, positive influences from the past.

Ljossalfheimr Light elf world, mental influences.

Midgardhr Middle earth, the querents relationship to the other realms (worlds).

Svartalfheimr Dark elf world (dwarves), creative and emotional influences for the present and the future.

Hel Realm of the dead, negative influences from the past.

Nifleheimr Realm of ice, restrictive outside influences.

Muspelheimr Realm of fire, active outside influences.

Vanaheimr Realm of water, the Vanir, balancing influences and emotional relationships.

Jotunheimr Realm of chaos, the Giants, unbalancing mental influences.

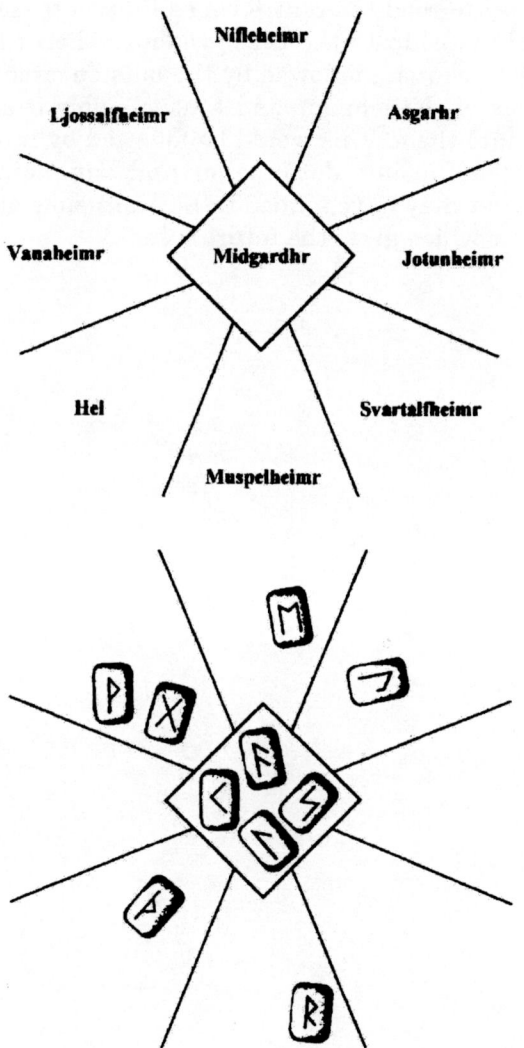

Fig 4

Reading
It is necessary to read the centre runes first as these give the querents relationship to the other realms. Then the realms from the past are read, followed by the outside circumstances in the realms of Nifleheimr and Muspelheimr if any runes have fallen into them. This would be followed by interpreting any runes that fall into Jotunheimr and Vanaheimr before looking at what may have landed in Ljossalfheimr and finally Svartalfheimr which gives the future trends.

Rune Spreads

Unlike the rune casts, the spreads can be layed out in specific patterns by choosing from three to nine runes, taken from a bag or suitable container. They must however be chosen intuitively without looking at them until they have all been laid out. The Question Spread, shown overleaf is useful for giving an answer to a yes or no question.

Fig 5

Once chosen, their are a number of possibilities that can occur due to some runes being reversible. The simple case is three upright or three reversed, meaning Yes or No respectively. A reversible rune does not change the result but does require that more thought must be used before a decision is made.

The Situation Spread is however to be interpreted using Past, Present and Future and can often be of great use if used in conjunction with other spreads or casts.

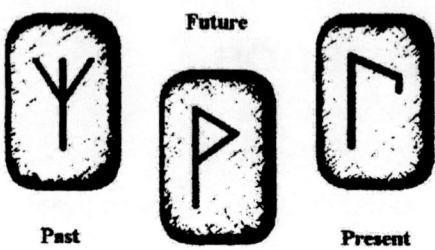

Fig 6

The situation spread can be expanded to create a spread called Valknutr Knot. Which in effect is three interconnecting triangles (see "At the Well of Wyrd" by Thorsson). A representation of this in the form of a spread is given in Fig 5.

Each group of three runes is associated with a Norn and can be read separately similar to the situation spread as well as vertically referring to the Past, Present and then the Future.

The last spread that is dealt with is called Mimirs Head and is a simple yet informative way of using only seven runes. It probes into a problem, giving the events leading up to it, and advice if the final outcome is to be realised or avoided.

The first six runes are laid out in 3 pairs of two with the seventh rune on its own, as shown in Fig 6.

A question need not be asked as the spread will usually outline the problem that is relevant to the querent at that time e.g. the querent is unsure about booking a holiday at this time.

Answer: Positions 1 and 2 refer to Hagalaz and Raidho, indicating that he is unsure because of outside circumstances

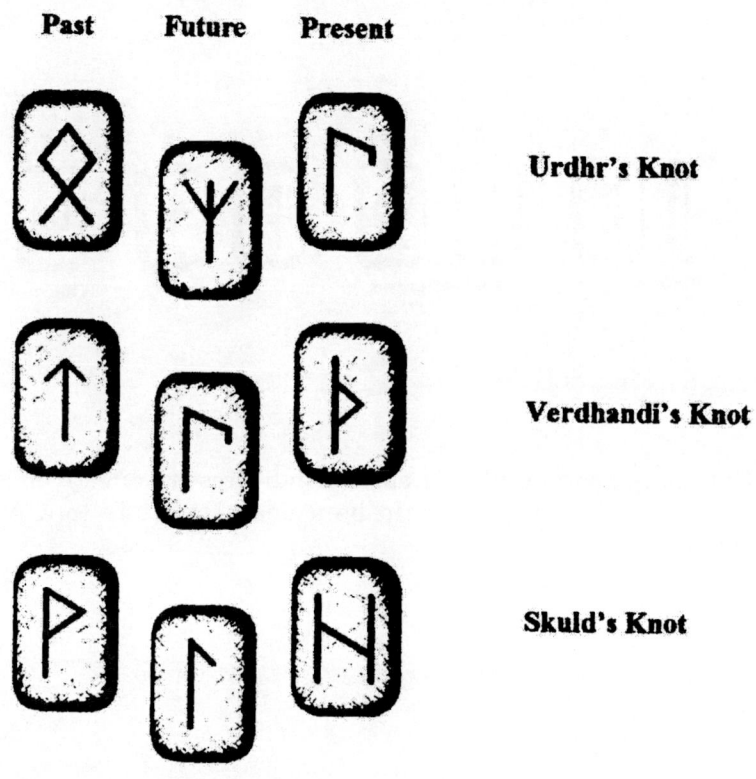

Fig 7   Valknutr Spread

around him at that time. Positions 3 and 4 are the runes Thurisaz and Othala and show that his unsurity is due to problems about his home life. The advice runes in position 5 and 6 are Wunjo and Nauthiz which are indicating a delay but that will eventually prove beneficial. This advice is strengthened by the outcome rune Sowilo that suggests that everything planned will be achieved.

Fig 8   Mimirs Head

The above reading of this spread indicates its effectiveness and versatility which would be a useful prelude to a full reading.

Advanced Divination

To understand divination in a more advanced form, some previous concepts need to be clarified, and new ideas added. Thus opening a vast reservoir of knowledge yet to be explored.

From chapter one we found that the soul/body could be divided into a number of different levels. Namely the Hamingja, Minni, Hugr, Hamr and the Lich, which when combined form the body as a whole.

These first become defined at the moment of birth or in some societies at the time of Naming. So that the persons name and date of birth are essential in describing the person. Thus we can use the runes and numerology to create a psychological reading that can be constantly updated and evaluated. It is for this reason that the symbol of the world serpent swallowing its tail is used and the reading is called Jormungands Tail.

Jormungands Tail

Having worked out a persons psyche at the time of birth we can do a reading based on its results at any time, allowing their progress or problems to be highlighted and dealt with accordingly.

For the purpose of example a fictious name is used and the following spread is drawn to be compared with the spread that is worked out for their time of birth.

ᚠ　　Hamingja
ᛒᛏᛋ　Minni
ᛋ　　Hugr
ᛏᛉᚾ　Hamr
ᚨ　　Lich

To work out the initial spread we begin with their date of birth and full name.

Initial Reading

Abbr.	Description	Level
DOB	Date of Birth	Hamingja
SNT	Separate Name Totals	Minni
NT	Name Total	Hugr
SNDB	Separate Name Totals and Date of Birth	Hamr
NTDB	Name Total & Date of Birth	Lich

Using 17th September 1958 as the birth date, we can obtain the following numerology.

1+7+9+1+9+5+8 = 40

Futher addition of the 4 and the 0 yields the fourth rune Ansuz(See appendix 2) and describes this persons Hamingja at his time of birth.

Proceeding through the levels to the Minni we need his full name, which is to be written in runic as follows.

Simon   ᛋᛁᛗᛟᚾ   16+11+20+23+10=80
Alfred   ᚨᛚᚠᚱᛖᛞ   4+21+1+5+19+24=74
Richards ᚱᛁᚲᚺᚨᚱᛞᛋ   5+11+6+9+4+5+24+16=80

From these numbers we can obtain the following runes for the level known as the Minni

80 - 8+0=8   ᚹ Wunjo
74 - 7+4=11 | Isa
80 - 8+0=8   ᚹ Wunjo

The spread is now easier to work out as we have completed all the groundwork. The rest is simple arithmetic.
For the Hugr we add the three separate name totals together to give the Name Total.

Name Total 80+74+80 = 234 - 2+3+4 = 9 Hagalaz

For the next two levels we need to use his date of birth in conjunction with the name totals. So that for the Hamr we add the separate name totals to the date of birth as follows.

SNT 80 + DOB 40 = 120 1+2+0 = 3 Thurisaz
SNT 74 + DOB 40 = 114 1+1+4 = 6 Kenaz

To complete this initial spread we add the Name Total to his Date of Birth, giving us the rune for the Lich.

NT 234 + DOB 40 +274 2+7+4 = 13 Eihwaz

To clarify the workings for the initial reading we can now compare it with the sample spread we looked at originally.

Initial	Sample	Level
ᚠ	ᚠ	Hamingja
ᚠᛁᚠ	ᛒᛏᛋ	Minni
ᚺ	ᛃ	Hugr
ᛏ᚜ᛏ	ᛏᚷᚾ	Hamr
ᛁ	ᚠ	Lich

Beginning with the Hamingja we compare the rune in each spread to each other. This shows that they are the same, that he is in harmony on this level with his true self. The other levels however are somewhat different but very positive.

The Minni shows that he is capable of many new ideas that can happen suddenly, and are likely to be successful. They are however tempered by the rune Jera in the Hugr, which suggests that he must wait to apply these ideas, to find the most opportune moment. This is in sharp contrast to his initial birth spread where due to the runes Isa and Hagalaz his own thoughts and memories were suppressed and replaced by those outside of him.

With the Hamr his emotions have changed from sharp destructive outbursts to a holding in with the rune Ingwaz but then using that emotional energy in a giving and positive way as shown by the runes Gyfu and Tiwaz.

The Lich represents how the other levels cooperate and it becomes the result of that. It manifests in our physical self and as to how other people perceive us. Here again this persons spread shows a change from an overly offensive attitude to one of fulfilment and energy that is gained by the rune Fehu. This then is a short example of how the reading of this spread can proceed.

Omens and Patterns

Wyrd is our personal web, it determines how we interact with the world. It is written from moment to moment and with awareness it can be worked with to improve our future. However it is often written in line with our Orlog, which is the impersonal web created by everything else but mainly by society. It is difficult to avoid and as such is thought of as Fate or Karma.

To see and use our wyrd, we must observe the patterns of life. This can be made easier by a form of divination using only nine stones or pieces of wood that can be located at the time the reading is required. As in the example below.

Fig 9

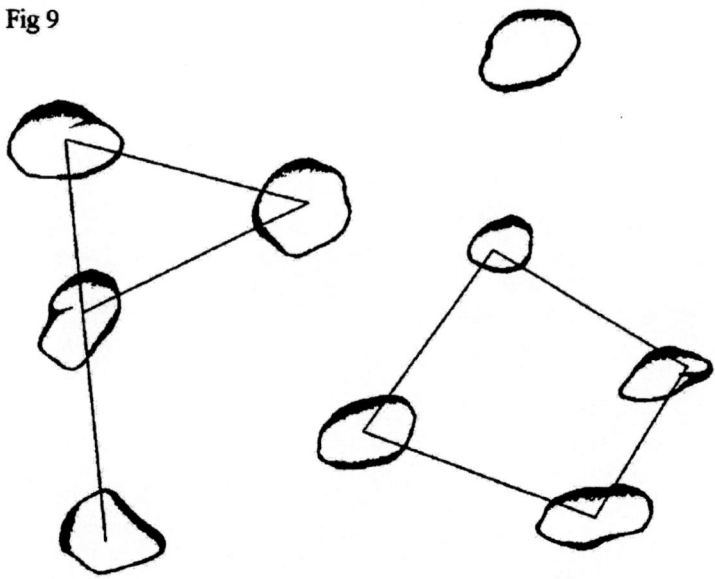

Their are two shapes most apparent in this cast, the runes Wunjo and Ingwaz. Their are however other shapes hidden within and they do not need to be runes to be of meaning.

Thus nature will provide a way of divination without the necessity of having ones own individual set of rune stones. Thus allowing the patterns and shapes surrounding us to be brought to our attention as a form of knowledge. Collectively these are known as Omens and are seen as spirals, circles, crosses, a bird in a tree, an animal crossing our path, almost anything that happens in a specific way, that will light our awareness to its nature. All has meaning if you are aware, so that the truth is bound only by your imagination, which knows no limits.

Glossary

Aegir/Ran	God and Goddess of the sea.
Aesir	Gods of the Air and War, they live in Asgardhr and is used as a general term for the Gods.
Angrboda	A giantess, with whom Loki sired three fearsome offspring, Hella, Jormungand and Fenris.
Aska	The first man, created from an ash tree and given life by Odhinn, Vili and Ve.
Austri	A dwarf charged by Odhinn to hold the eastern corner of the sky for always.
Audmula	The great cow that emerged before all else from the blocks of ice that are the realm of Nifleheimr.
Balder	A sun god who was killed by an arrow made from Mistletoe, only to rise from Hel after Ragnarok.
Dokkalfar	Mound elves that look after the harvest and are generally helpful, as well as being well versed inmagic.
Embla	The first woman, created from an elm tree and given life by Odhinn and his brothers.
Etin	A wise ageless being formed when the worlds were first created.
Fenris	An offspring of Loki that was eventually bound by a magical cord "Glaupnir". It was during this task that Tyr lost his hand (see section on mythology).
Fetch	Part of the soul that can be in animal female form.
Forseti	Son of Baldur and the God of justice to men and gods alike.

Freya	Sister of Yngvi Freyr, she is the goddess of fertility and sexual pleasure. Freya is the magical consort of Odhinn and is identified with the teachings of seidh-magic.
Frigga	The wife of Odhinn and the goddess of marriage and childbirth.
Futhark	A term used to describe the language known as Runic.
Ginnungap	A void that separates the realms of Fire and Ice.
Hamingja	The innermost self revealed to be the life force also known as mana or personal luck.
Hamr	The emotional or astral self that creates the Lich or Shield Skin.
Heimdallr	Father of the human race, protector of the gods. He hears all in the same way Odhinn sees all as he keeps guard over bifröst and will sound the horn "Gjallarhorn" to signal the coming of Ragnarok.
Hella	Ruler of Hel, she has the appearance of a beautiful woman above and of a rotting corpse below the waist.
Hugr	The Hugr relates to our thoughts and connects with one of Odhinn's ravens Huginn.
Hverglmir	One of the three wells of wyrd this one can be found in Nifleheimr next to the third root of the world tree.
Innangardhr	An area consisting of Midgardhr, Ljossalfheimr, and Svartalfheimr.
Jormungand	An immense serpent that encircles Midgardhr, swallowing it own tail in the process.
Lich	The physical self, the Sheild Skin it encloses all aspects of the self.
Loki	Brother of Odhinn, he was the god of chaos and mischief. Bringing about Baldur's death and being instrumental in causing the downfall of the gods at Ragnarok.

Mani	A god that carries the spark of the moon from Muspelheimr across the sky in a chariot whilst being chased by the wolf Hati.
Minni	Part of the mind known as the memory it is the complement to the Hugr.
Njord	The god of the sea he once married a giantess Skadhi.
Nordri	The dwarf that holds the northern corner of the sky.
Norns	The Three sisters of fate Urd, Verdhandi and Skuld.
Ogham	Celtic tree runes, so named as each letter was associated with a tree.
Odhinn	Allfather of the gods and the giver of the runes.
Ohdrerir	The divine mead of poetry that gives inspiration to all poetic forms.
Ragnarok	Twilight of the Old Gods. A great battle called Ragnarok destroys the old gods allowing their sons and daughters to follow on from them into a new age.
Rune	A symbolic name for the letters of the Futhark that suggests hidden mysteries found within the Runic alphabet.
Seidhr	Shamanic magic used by Rune magicians.
Sif	Wife of Thorr, goddess of fertility. Her golden hair represents the corn harvest.
Skald	The name for a travelling poet/storyteller.
Skuld	The Norn of the future, she can be pictured as a young veiled female.
Sleipnir	Odhinn's eight legged steed, fathered by Loki.
Sol	Chased by the wolf Skoll, Sol carries the sun across the sky in a chariot.
Stave	A small block of wood or stone that has a rune symbol carved or painted onto it.
Sudri	The southern dwarf.
Thorr	God of thunder and defender of the gods against the Giants.

Tyr	God of war, he lost his hand in the binding of the wolf Fenris.
Urd	The Norn of the past, the old Hag, she combines the strands of the web ready for Verdhandi.
Vanir	Gods that reside in Vanaheimr. They are concerned with fertility, death and Seidhr magic.
Verdhandi	The Norn of the present, she weaves the web which is unpicked again by Skuld. Verdhandi is pregnant with that which is now.
Ve	One of Odhinn's brothers.
Vestri	The western dwarf.
Vili	One of Odhinns brother, known as the will.
Vitki	A rune magician or seeress.
Wyrd	The web of fate that is continually spun, determining a persons path from birth to death.
Ymir	Protobeing who was sacrificed to create the nine worlds from his body, as described in the Havámal.
Yngvi Freyr	The brother of Freya and likewise a god of fertility.

Bibliography

Aswynn, Freya, "*Leaves of Yggdrasil*"
Barrett, Clive, "*The Norse Tarot*"
Bates, Brian, "*The Way of Wyrd*"
Bunney, Sarah, "*The Illustrated Encyclopaedia of Herbs*"
Crossley-Holland, Kevin, "*The Norse Myths*"
Crossley-Holland, Kevin, "*Axe Age, Wolf Age*"
Crowley, Aleister, "*777 and other Qabilistic writings*"
Culpeper, Nicholas, "*Culpepers Complete Herbal*"
Davison, H.R.Ellis, "*Gods and Myths of Northern Europe*"
Evans, D.H., "*Germania by Tacitus*"
Grant, John, "*An introduction to Viking Mythology*"
Graves, Robert, "*The White Goddess*"
Gundarsson, Kvelduf, "*Teutonic Magic*"
Howard, Micheal, "*The Wisdom of the Runes*"
Millard/Evans , "*The Usborne Book of Norse Legends*"
Monsen, Erling, "*Heimskringla - The lives of the Norse Kings*"
Page, R.I., "*Reading the Past, Runes*"
Peschel, Lisa, "*A Practical Guide to the Runes*"
Picard, Barbara-Leoni, "*Tales of the Norse Gods and Heroes*"
Simpson, Jacqueline, "*Everyday Life in the Viking Age*"
Taylor, W.B., "*Poetic Edda*"
Thorsson, Edred, "*At the Well of Wyrd*"
Thorsson, Edred, "*Runelore*"
Titchenell, Elsa-Brita, "*The Masks of Odhinn*"

Appendix 1

Rune	Tree	God	Element
Fehu	Elder	Freya	Earth/Fire
Uruz	Birch	Dokkalfar	Earth
Thurisaz	Oak	Thorr	Air
Ansuz	Ash	Odhinn	Air
Raidho	Hazel/Oak	Forsetti	Air
Kenaz	Pine	Freya	Fire
Gyfu	Ash/Elm	Odhinn	Earth
Wunjo	Hazel	Baldur	Fire
Hagalaz	Yew	Urd/Hella	Water/Ice
Nauthiz	Beech	Skuld	Fire
Isa	Alder	Verdhandi	Water/Ice
Jera	Apple	Sif	Earth
Eihwaz	Yew	Hella	Earth
Perthro	Ash	Norns	Water
Elhaz	Ash	Heimdallr	Air
Sowilo	Juniper	Sol	Fire
Tiwaz	Oak	Tyr	Air
Berkano	Birch	Frigga	Earth/Water
Ehwaz	Oak/Ash	Sleipnir	Earth/Air
Mannaz	Holly	Manni	Air
Laguz	Willow	Njord	Water
Ingwaz	Apple	Yngvi Freyr	Earth/Water
Othala	Oak	Heimdallr	Earth
Dagaz	Alder	Baldur	Fire

Appendix 2

No	Rune Symbol	Rune Name	Meaning
1	ᚠ	Fehu	Cattle
2	ᚢ	Uruz	Wild Aurochs
3	ᚦ	Thurisaz	Giant, Thorn
4	ᚨ	Ansuz	God, Odhinn
5	ᚱ	Raidho	Cart, Sunwheel
6	ᚲ	Kenaz	Torch
7	ᚷ	Gyfu	Gift
8	ᚹ	Wunjo	Joy, Harmony
9	ᚺ	Hagalaz	Hailstones
10	ᚾ	Nauthiz	Need, Necessity
11	ᛁ	Isa	Ice
12	ᛃ	Jera	Harvest, Year
13	ᛇ	Eihwaz	Yew Tree
14	ᛈ	Perthro	Lot Box
15	ᛉ	Elhaz	Elk
16	ᛊ	Sowilo	Sun
17	ᛏ	Tiwaz	God Tyr
18	ᛒ	Berkano	Birch Tree
19	ᛖ	Ehwaz	Horse
20	ᛗ	Mannaz	God Mannus, People
21	ᛚ	Laguz	Water
22	ᛜ	Ingwaz	God Freyr
23	ᛟ	Othala	Odal Land
24	ᛞ	Dagaz	Day

Appendix 3

Pronunciation Guide

To aid the pronunciation of the rune names, and of old Norse, the following two guides have been included.

Rune Names

    a - as in "father"
    e - ay, as in "day"
    i - ee, as in "speed"
    o - as in "home"
    u - oo, as in "moon"
    dh - a soft th, as in "leather"
    g - always hard, as in "give"
    h - ch, as in "choke"
    j - always pronounced as a y
    k - always hard, never a soft c
    th - as in "thorn"
    z - always buzzed, between an r and a z

Old Norse

    a - as in "law"
    a - as in "father"
    e - as i in "gin"
    e - as ay in "day"
    i - as in "is"
    i - ee as in "speed"
    o - as in "omit"

o - as in "owe"
o,o - as in "not"
u - oo, as in "soot"
u - oo, as in "droop"
y - u, as in French tu
y - u, as in German Tur
ae - e as in "get"
au - ou as in "house"
ei - ay as in "day"
ey - as ei
dh - a soft th, as in "leather"
f - as in English but as a v in medial and end positions
g - as in "give"
j - always as a y
ng – as in "sing"
r - trilled
s - as in "blast"
th - as in "thorn"
R - pronounced as between a 'z' and an 'r'

Other titles published by Capall Bann:

Rune Rede, Wisdom and Magic for the Life Journey by Ruarik Grimnisson

This book incorporates the essentials that are common to those cultures where Runes were used, and remains true to their Heathen origins. The Runic 'alphabets' were not just a system of writing for the Germanic peoples - they were a Life-Code. Encrypted in their numerical ordering and individual symbolism is a guide to the life journey of the soul - a holistic approach for the individual and collective folk to survive and thrive in the worlds of nature, mankind and the spiritual realms. Their magick arose from the understanding of the inseparability of all phenomena - what our ancestors called the Wyrd. This book presents an integrated collection of basic Rune Lore in the manner the author believes it was meant to be given - as a counsel for the soul's life journey. This book contains the codes that will make the way clear. For those who are seeking insight into the psychological world of our pre-industrial ancestors, this book will reveal to you their basic attitudes and expectations. The ancestral mythology interwoven with each rune-rede is presented for your own contemplation. Study of the knowledge herein seen through the lens of heathen understanding will reveal an alternative map of reality that will aid you on your life journey.   ISBN 186163 126X   £14.95

The Northern Tradition   by Pete Jennings

"Written by the President of the Pagan Federation, who is also a follower of the Norse (or Northern) Tradition - so he can be classed as a bit of an authority on the subject. A good basic introduction to anyone interested in finding out about this particular Pagan path." Dragonsphere   "Pete has clearly set out the basic principles of the Norse Tradition" Wiccan Rede   "A compact, concise, very affordable book that I would have no hesitation in recommending" Eastern Spirit. A comprehensive introduction to the Northern Tradition, a vibrant, living current within the multitude of spiritual paths of Paganism. It explains the Pagan religious beliefs of the Saxon and Norse peoples and their associated magic. Through practical exercises the book teaches you about runes, Troth, folklore and rituals in addition to the history of this exciting and mysterious tradition and it's practise and relevance today. Enhanced by illustrations by Jane Brideson of Dark Moon Designs   ISBN 186163 1871   £7.95

The Book of Seidr - The Native English and Northern European Shamanic Tradition by Runic John

Seidr is the ancient Northern European shamanism. The main practice of seidr, as with all shamanic traditions, is the use of various extremely ancient techniques to affect the mind and alter our consciousness to a state in which we can perceive and work with the hidden realm of spirit directly. We may take up the practice of Seidr initially for ourselves to give us a better understanding of ourselves and of the hidden realm that normally lurks beneath the onion skin we call reality. We can use seidr to connect on a deeper level to our own inner self and to enhance our particular skills and positive qualities. Seidr can also help us to connect to the hidden realms of nature on a before unimaginable depth, allowing us to gain an experiential understanding of the natural world and all that dwell therein; to actually feel one with the forest, the earth and the sky. Through seidr you may truly begin to form a real relationship with our ancestors and the elder gods and goddesses of our folk. As you embark on this path of seidr, never again will the world look empty and hollow, for your eyes will learn to see the spirit in all things and to hear the voices of the ancient ones.   ISBN 186163 2290

FREE DETAILED CATALOGUE

Capall Bann is owned and run by people actively involved in many of the areas in which we publish. A detailed illustrated catalogue is available on request, SAE or International Postal Coupon appreciated. **Titles can be ordered direct from Capall Bann, post free in the UK** (cheque or PO with order) or from good bookshops and specialist outlets.

A Breath Behind Time, Terri Hector
Angels and Goddesses - Celtic Christianity & Paganism, M. Howard
Arthur - The Legend Unveiled, C Johnson & E Lung
Astrology The Inner Eye - A Guide in Everyday Language, E Smith
Auguries and Omens - The Magical Lore of Birds, Yvonne Aburrow
Asyniur - Womens Mysteries in the Northern Tradition, S McGrath
Beginnings - Geomancy, Builder's Rites & Electional Astrology in the European Tradition, Nigel Pennick
Between Earth and Sky, Julia Day
Book of the Veil , Peter Paddon
Caer Sidhe - Celtic Astrology and Astronomy, Vol 1, Michael Bayley
Caer Sidhe - Celtic Astrology and Astronomy, Vol 2 M Bayley
Call of the Horned Piper, Nigel Jackson
Cat's Company, Ann Walker
Celtic Faery Shamanism, Catrin James
Celtic Faery Shamanism - The Wisdom of the Otherworld, Catrin James
Celtic Lore & Druidic Ritual, Rhiannon Ryall
Celtic Sacrifice - Pre Christian Ritual & Religion, Marion Pearce
Celtic Saints and the Glastonbury Zodiac, Mary Caine
Circle and the Square, Jack Gale
Compleat Vampyre - The Vampyre Shaman, Nigel Jackson
Creating Form From the Mist - The Wisdom of Women in Celtic Myth and Culture, Lynne Sinclair-Wood
Crystal Clear - A Guide to Quartz Crystal, Jennifer Dent
Crystal Doorways, Simon & Sue Lilly
Crossing the Borderlines - Guising, Masking & Ritual Animal Disguise in the European Tradition, Nigel Pennick
Dragons of the West, Nigel Pennick
Earth Dance - A Year of Pagan Rituals, Jan Brodie
Earth Harmony - Places of Power, Holiness & Healing, Nigel Pennick
Earth Magic, Margaret McArthur
Eildon Tree (The) Romany Language & Lore, Michael Hoadley

Enchanted Forest - The Magical Lore of Trees, Yvonne Aburrow
Eternal Priestess, Sage Weston
Eternally Yours Faithfully, Roy Radford & Evelyn Gregory
Everything You Always Wanted To Know About Your Body, But So Far Nobody's Been Able To Tell You, Chris Thomas & D Baker
Face of the Deep - Healing Body & Soul, Penny Allen
Fairies in the Irish Tradition, Molly Gowen
Familiars - Animal Powers of Britain, Anna Franklin
Fool's First Steps, (The) Chris Thomas
Forest Paths - Tree Divination, Brian Harrison, Ill. S. Rouse
From Past to Future Life, Dr Roger Webber
Gardening For Wildlife Ron Wilson
God Year, The, Nigel Pennick & Helen Field
Goddess on the Cross, Dr George Young
Goddess Year, The, Nigel Pennick & Helen Field
Goddesses, Guardians & Groves, Jack Gale
Handbook For Pagan Healers, Liz Joan
Handbook of Fairies, Ronan Coghlan
Healing Book, The, Chris Thomas and Diane Baker
Healing Homes, Jennifer Dent
Healing Journeys, Paul Williamson
Healing Stones, Sue Philips
Herb Craft - Shamanic & Ritual Use of Herbs, Lavender & Franklin
Hidden Heritage - Exploring Ancient Essex, Terry Johnson
Hub of the Wheel, Skytoucher
In Search of Herne the Hunter, Eric Fitch
Inner Celtia, Alan Richardson & David Annwn
Inner Mysteries of the Goths, Nigel Pennick
Inner Space Workbook - Develop Thru Tarot, C Summers & J Vayne
Intuitive Journey, Ann Walker Isis - African Queen, Akkadia Ford
Journey Home, The, Chris Thomas
Kecks, Keddles & Kesh - Celtic Lang & The Cog Almanac, Bayley
Language of the Psycards, Berenice
Legend of Robin Hood, The, Richard Rutherford-Moore
Lid Off the Cauldron, Patricia Crowther
Light From the Shadows - Modern Traditional Witchcraft, Gwyn
Living Tarot, Ann Walker
Lore of the Sacred Horse, Marion Davies
Lost Lands & Sunken Cities (2nd ed.), Nigel Pennick
Magic of Herbs - A Complete Home Herbal, Rhiannon Ryall
Magical Guardians - Exploring the Spirit and Nature of Trees, Philip Heselton
Magical History of the Horse, Janet Farrar & Virginia Russell
Magical Lore of Animals, Yvonne Aburrow
Magical Lore of Cats, Marion Davies
Magical Lore of Herbs, Marion Davies
Magick Without Peers, Ariadne Rainbird & David Rankine

Masks of Misrule - Horned God & His Cult in Europe, Nigel Jackson
Medicine For The Coming Age, Lisa Sand MD
Medium Rare - Reminiscences of a Clairvoyant, Muriel Renard
Menopausal Woman on the Run, Jaki da Costa
Mind Massage - 60 Creative Visualisations, Marlene Maundrill
Mirrors of Magic - Evoking the Spirit of the Dewponds, P Heselton
Moon Mysteries, Jan Brodie
Mysteries of the Runes, Michael Howard
Mystic Life of Animals, Ann Walker
New Celtic Oracle The, Nigel Pennick & Nigel Jackson
Oracle of Geomancy, Nigel Pennick
Pagan Feasts - Seasonal Food for the 8 Festivals, Franklin & Phillips
Patchwork of Magic - Living in a Pagan World, Julia Day
Pathworking - A Practical Book of Guided Meditations, Pete Jennings
Personal Power, Anna Franklin
Pickingill Papers - The Origins of Gardnerian Wicca, Bill Liddell
Pillars of Tubal Cain, Nigel Jackson
Places of Pilgrimage and Healing, Adrian Cooper
Practical Divining, Richard Foord
Practical Meditation, Steve Hounsome
Practical Spirituality, Steve Hounsome
Psychic Self Defence - Real Solutions, Jan Brodie
Real Fairies, David Tame
Reality - How It Works & Why It Mostly Doesn't, Rik Dent
Romany Tapestry, Michael Houghton
Rune Rede, Ruric Grimnisson
Runic Astrology, Nigel Pennick
Sacred Animals, Gordon MacLellan
Sacred Celtic Animals, Marion Davies, Ill. Simon Rouse
Sacred Dorset - On the Path of the Dragon, Peter Knight
Sacred Grove - The Mysteries of the Forest, Yvonne Aburrow
Sacred Geometry, Nigel Pennick
Sacred Nature, Ancient Wisdom & Modern Meanings, A Cooper
Sacred Ring - Pagan Origins of British Folk Festivals, M. Howard
Season of Sorcery - On Becoming a Wisewoman, Poppy Palin
Seasonal Magic - Diary of a Village Witch, Paddy Slade
Secret Places of the Goddess, Philip Heselton
Secret Signs & Sigils, Nigel Pennick
Self Enlightenment, Mayan O'Brien
Spirits of the Air, Jaq D Hawkins
Spirits of the Earth, Jaq D Hawkins
Stony Gaze, Investigating Celtic Heads John Billingsley
Stumbling Through the Undergrowth , Mark Kirwan-Heyhoe
Subterranean Kingdom, The, revised 2nd ed, Nigel Pennick
Symbols of Ancient Gods, Rhiannon Ryall
Talking to the Earth, Gordon MacLellan

Taming the Wolf - Full Moon Meditations, Steve Hounsome
Teachings of the Wisewomen, Rhiannon Ryall
The Other Kingdoms Speak, Helena Hawley
Tree: Essence of Healing, Simon & Sue Lilly
Tree: Essence, Spirit & Teacher, Simon & Sue Lilly
Through the Veil, Peter Paddon
Torch and the Spear, Patrick Regan
Understanding Chaos Magic, Jaq D Hawkins
Vortex - The End of History, Mary Russell
Warp and Weft - In Search of the I-Ching, William de Fancourt
Warriors at the Edge of Time, Jan Fry
Water Witches, Tony Steele
Way of the Magus, Michael Howard
Weaving a Web of Magic, Rhiannon Ryall
West Country Wicca, Rhiannon Ryall
Wildwitch - The Craft of the Natural Psychic, Poppy Palin
Wildwood King , Philip Kane
Witches of Oz, Matthew & Julia Philips
Wondrous Land - The Faery Faith of Ireland by Dr Kay Mullin
Working With the Merlin, Geoff Hughes
Your Talking Pet, Ann Walker

FREE detailed catalogue and FREE 'Inspiration' magazine

Contact: Capall Bann Publishing, Auton Farm, Milverton, Somerset, TA4 1NE